Buddhist Guidelines to Skillful Communication: Discourses from Anguttara Nikaya

Bodhi Path Press

GRAPEVINE INDIA

Published by

GRAPEVINE INDIA PUBLISHERS PVT LTD

www.grapevineindia.com

Delhi | Mumbai

email: grapevineindiapublishers@gmail.com

Ordering Information:

Quantity sales: Special discounts are available on quantity

purchases by corporations, associations, and others.

For details, reach out to the publisher.

First published by Grapevine India 2024

APARAACCHARASAṄGHATAVAGGA:

Another Chapter on a Finger-Snap

394

"If, mendicants, a mendicant develops the first absorption, even as long as a finger-snap, they are called

a mendicant who does not lack absorption, who follows the Teacher's instructions, who responds to advice, and who does not eat the country's alms in vain.

How much more so those who make much of it!"

395–401

"If, mendicants, a mendicant develops the second …

third …

or fourth absorption …

or the heart's release by love …

or the heart's release by compassion …

or the heart's release by rejoicing …

or the heart's release by equanimity, even as long as a finger-snap …

402–405

If a mendicant meditates by observing an aspect of the body …

feelings …

mind …

principles—keen, aware, and mindful, rid of desire and aversion for the world, even for the time of a finger-snap …

406–409

If they generate enthusiasm, try, make an effort, exert the mind, and strive so that bad, unskillful qualities don't arise, even for the time of a finger-snap …

If they generate enthusiasm, try, make an effort, exert the mind, and strive so that bad, unskillful qualities that have arisen are given up, even for the time of a finger-snap …

If they generate enthusiasm, try, make an effort, exert the mind, and strive so that skillful qualities that have not arisen do arise, even for the time of a finger-snap …

If they generate enthusiasm, try, make an effort, exert the mind, and strive so that skillful qualities that have arisen remain, are not lost, but increase, mature, and are fulfilled by development, even for the time of a finger-snap …

410–413

If they develop the basis of psychic power that has immersion due to enthusiasm, and active effort …

the basis of psychic power that has immersion due to energy, and active effort …

the basis of psychic power that has immersion due to mental development, and active effort …

the basis of psychic power that has immersion due to inquiry, and active effort, even for the time of a finger-snap …

414–418

If they develop the faculty of faith …

the faculty of energy …

the faculty of mindfulness …

the faculty of immersion …

the faculty of wisdom, even for the time of a finger-snap …

419–423

If they develop the power of faith …

the power of energy …

the power of mindfulness …

the power of immersion …

the power of wisdom, even for the time of a finger-snap …

424–430

If they develop the awakening factor of mindfulness …

the awakening factor of investigation of principles …

the awakening factor of energy …

the awakening factor of rapture …

the awakening factor of tranquility …

the awakening factor of immersion …

the awakening factor of equanimity, even for the time of a finger-snap …

431–438

If they develop right view …

right thought …

right speech …

right action …

right livelihood …

right effort …

right mindfulness …

right immersion, even for the time of a finger-snap …

Perceiving form internally, they see visions externally, limited, both pretty and ugly.

Having mastered this, they are aware that:

'I know and see.' …

Perceiving form internally, they see visions externally, limitless, both pretty and ugly.

Having mastered this, they are aware that:

'I know and see.' …

Not perceiving form internally, they see visions externally, limited, both pretty and ugly.

Having mastered this, they are aware that:

'I know and see.' …

Not perceiving form internally, they see visions externally, limitless, both pretty and ugly.

Having mastered this, they are aware that:

'I know and see.' …

Not perceiving form internally, they see visions externally that are blue, with blue color, blue hue, and blue tint.

Having mastered this, they are aware that:

'I know and see.' …

Not perceiving form internally, they see visions externally that are yellow, with yellow color, yellow hue, and yellow tint.

Having mastered this, they are aware that:

'I know and see.' …

Not perceiving form internally, they see visions externally that are red, with red color, red hue, and red tint.

Having mastered this, they are aware that:

'I know and see.' …

Not perceiving form internally, they see visions externally that are white, with white color, white hue, and white tint.

Having mastered this, they are aware that:

'I know and see.' …

447–454

Having physical form, they see visions …

not perceiving form internally, they see visions externally …

they're focused only on beauty …

going totally beyond perceptions of form, with the ending of perceptions of impingement, not focusing on perceptions of diversity, aware that 'space is infinite', they enter and remain in the dimension of infinite space …

going totally beyond the dimension of infinite space, aware that 'consciousness is infinite', they enter and remain in the dimension of infinite consciousness …

going totally beyond the dimension of infinite consciousness, aware that 'there is nothing at all', they enter and remain in the dimension of nothingness …

going totally beyond the dimension of nothingness, they enter and remain in the dimension of neither perception nor non-perception …

going totally beyond the dimension of neither perception nor non-perception, they enter and remain in the cessation of perception and feeling …

455–464

They develop the meditation on universal earth …

the meditation on universal water …

the meditation on universal fire …

the meditation on universal air …

the meditation on universal blue …

the meditation on universal yellow …

the meditation on universal red …

the meditation on universal white …

the meditation on universal space …

the meditation on universal consciousness …

465–474

They develop the perception of ugliness …

the perception of death …

the perception of the repulsiveness of food …

the perception of dissatisfaction with the whole world …

the perception of impermanence …

the perception of suffering in impermanence …

the perception of not-self in suffering …

the perception of giving up …

the perception of fading away …

the perception of cessation …

475–484

They develop the perception of impermanence …

the perception of not-self …

the perception of death …

the perception of the repulsiveness of food …

the perception of dissatisfaction with the whole world …

the perception of a skeleton …

the perception of the worm-infested corpse …

the perception of the livid corpse …

the perception of the split open corpse …

the perception of the bloated corpse …

485–494

They develop the recollection of the Buddha …

the recollection of the teaching …

the recollection of the Saṅgha …

the recollection of ethical conduct …

the recollection of generosity …

the recollection of the deities …

mindfulness of breathing …

the recollection of death …

mindfulness of the body …

the recollection of peace …

495–574

They develop the faculty of faith together with the first absorption …

the faculty of energy …

the faculty of mindfulness …

the faculty of immersion …

the faculty of wisdom …

the power of faith …

the power of energy …

the power of mindfulness …

the power of immersion …

the power of wisdom together with the first absorption …

Together with the second absorption …

the third absorption …

the fourth absorption …

love …

compassion …

rejoicing …

They develop the faculty of faith together with equanimity …

They develop the faculty of energy …

the faculty of mindfulness …

the faculty of immersion …

the faculty of wisdom …

the power of faith …

the power of energy …

the power of mindfulness …

the power of immersion …

the power of wisdom.

That mendicant is called

a mendicant who does not lack absorption, who follows the Teacher's instructions, who responds to advice, and who does not eat the country's alms in vain.

How much more so those who make much of it!"

Sammaditthisutta:

Right View

"Mendicants, these four people are found in the world.

What four?

The confirmed ascetic, the white lotus ascetic, the pink lotus ascetic, and the exquisite ascetic of ascetics.

And how is a person a confirmed ascetic?

It's when a mendicant has right view, right thought, right speech, right action, right livelihood, right effort, right mindfulness, and right immersion.

That's how a person is a confirmed ascetic.

And how is a person a white lotus ascetic?

It's when they have right view, right thought, right speech, right action, right livelihood, right effort, right mindfulness, right immersion, right knowledge, and right freedom. But they don't have direct meditative experience of the eight liberations.

That's how a person is a white lotus ascetic.

And how is a person a pink lotus ascetic?

It's when they have right view … and right freedom. And they do have direct meditative experience of the eight liberations.

That's how a person is a pink lotus ascetic.

And how is a person an exquisite ascetic of ascetics?

It's when a mendicant usually uses only what they've been invited to accept … And if anyone should be rightly called an exquisite ascetic of ascetics, it's me.

These arc the four people found in the world."

ATTHAṄGIKASUTTA:

Eightfold

"Mendicants, I will teach you a bad person and a worse person,

a good person and a better person.

And what is a bad person?

It's someone who has wrong view, wrong thought, wrong speech, wrong action, wrong livelihood, wrong effort, wrong mindfulness, and wrong immersion.

This is called a bad person.

And what is a worse person?

It's someone who has wrong view, wrong thought, wrong speech, wrong action, wrong livelihood, wrong effort, wrong mindfulness, and wrong immersion. And they encourage others in these same qualities.

This is called a worse person.

And what is a good person?

It's someone who has right view, right thought, right speech, right action, right livelihood, right effort, right mindfulness, and right immersion.

This is called a good person.

And what is a better person?

It's someone who has right view, right thought, right speech, right action, right livelihood, right effort, right mindfulness, and right immersion. And they encourage others in these same qualities.

This is called a better person."

DASAMAGGASUTTA:

The Path with Ten Factors

"Mendicants, I will teach you a bad person and a worse person,

a good person and a better person.

And what is a bad person?

It's someone who has wrong view, wrong thought, wrong speech, wrong action, wrong livelihood, wrong effort, wrong mindfulness, wrong immersion, wrong knowledge, and wrong freedom.

This is called a bad person.

And what is a worse person?

It's someone who has wrong view, wrong thought, wrong speech, wrong action, wrong livelihood, wrong effort, wrong mindfulness, wrong immersion, wrong knowledge, and wrong freedom. And they encourage others in these same qualities.

This is called a worse person.

And what is a good person?

It's someone who has right view, right thought, right speech, right action, right livelihood, right effort, right mindfulness, right immersion, right knowledge, and right freedom.

This is called a good person.

And what is a better person?

It's someone who has right view, right thought, right speech, right action, right livelihood, right effort, right mindfulness, right immersion, right knowledge, and right freedom. And they encourage others in these same qualities.

This is called a better person."

DUTIYAPAPADHAMMASUTTA:

Bad Character (2nd)

"Mendicants, I will teach you who's bad and who's worse,

who's good and who's better.

And who's bad?

It's someone who has wrong view, wrong thought, wrong speech, wrong action, wrong livelihood, wrong effort, wrong mindfulness, wrong immersion, wrong knowledge, and wrong freedom.

This is called bad.

And who's worse?

It's someone who has wrong view, wrong thought, wrong speech, wrong action, wrong livelihood, wrong effort, wrong mindfulness, wrong immersion, wrong knowledge, and wrong freedom. And they encourage others in these same qualities.

This is called worse.

And who's good?

It's someone who has right view, right thought, right speech, right action, right livelihood, right effort, right mindfulness, right immersion, right knowledge, and right freedom.

This is called good.

And who's better?

It's someone who has right view, right thought, right speech, right action, right livelihood, right effort, right mindfulness, right immersion, right knowledge, and right freedom. And they encourage others in these same qualities.

This is called better."

CATUTTHAPAPADHAMMASUTTA:

Bad Character (4th)

"Mendicants, I will teach you bad character and worse character,

good character and better character.

And who has bad character?

It's someone who has wrong view, wrong thought, wrong speech, wrong action, wrong livelihood, wrong effort, wrong mindfulness, wrong immersion, wrong knowledge, and wrong freedom.

This is called bad character.

And who has worse character?

It's someone who has wrong view, wrong thought, wrong speech, wrong action, wrong livelihood, wrong effort, wrong mindfulness, wrong immersion, wrong knowledge, and wrong freedom. And they encourage others in these same qualities.

This is called worse character.

And who has good character?

It's someone who has right view, right thought, right speech, right action, right livelihood, right effort, right mindfulness, right immersion, right knowledge, and right freedom.

This is called good character.

And who has better character?

It's someone who has right view, right thought, right speech, right action, right livelihood, right effort, right mindfulness, right immersion, right knowledge, and right freedom. And they encourage others in these same qualities.

This is called better character."

ARIYAMAGGASUTTA:

The Noble Path

"Mendicants, I declare these four kinds of deeds, having realized them with my own insight.

What four?

There are dark deeds with dark results;

bright deeds with bright results;

dark and bright deeds with dark and bright results; and

neither dark nor bright deeds with neither dark nor bright results, which lead to the ending of deeds.

And what are dark deeds with dark results?

It's when someone makes hurtful choices by way of body, speech, and mind. These are called dark deeds with dark results.

And what are bright deeds with bright results?

It's when someone makes pleasing choices by way of body, speech, and mind. These are called bright deeds with bright results.

And what are dark and bright deeds with dark and bright results?

It's when someone makes both hurtful and pleasing choices by way of body, speech, and mind. These are called dark and bright deeds with dark and bright results.

And what are neither dark nor bright deeds with neither dark nor bright results, which lead to the ending of deeds?

Right view, right thought, right speech, right action, right livelihood, right effort, right mindfulness, and right immersion.

These are called neither dark nor bright deeds with neither dark nor bright results, which lead to the ending of deeds.

These are the four kinds of deeds that I declare, having realized them with my own insight."

NIBBEDHIKASUTTA:

Penetrative

"Mendicants, I will teach you a penetrative exposition of the teaching.

Listen and pay close attention, I will speak."

"Yes, sir," they replied.

The Buddha said this:

"Mendicants, what is the penetrative exposition of the teaching?

Sensual pleasures should be known. And their source, diversity, result, cessation, and the practice that leads to their cessation should be known.

Feelings should be known. And their source, diversity, result, cessation, and the practice that leads to their cessation should be known.

Perceptions should be known. And their source, diversity, result, cessation, and the practice that leads to their cessation should be known.

Defilements should be known. And their source, diversity, result, cessation, and the practice that leads to their cessation should be known.

Deeds should be known. And their source, diversity, result, cessation, and the practice that leads to their cessation should be known.

Suffering should be known. And its source, diversity, result, cessation, and the practice that leads to its cessation should be known.

'Sensual pleasures should be known. And their source, diversity, result, cessation, and the practice that leads to their cessation should be known.' That's what I said,

but why did I say it?

There are these five kinds of sensual stimulation.

Sights known by the eye that are likable, desirable, agreeable, pleasant, sensual, and arousing.

Sounds known by the ear ...

Smells known by the nose ...

Tastes known by the tongue ...

Touches known by the body that are likable, desirable, agreeable, pleasant, sensual, and arousing.

However, these are not sensual pleasures. In the training of the Noble One they're called 'kinds of sensual stimulation'.

Greedy intention is a person's sensual pleasure.

The world's pretty things aren't sensual pleasures.

Greedy intention is a person's sensual pleasure.

The world's pretty things stay just as they are,

but a wise one removes desire for them.

And what is the source of sensual pleasures?

Contact is their source.

And what is the diversity of sensual pleasures?

The sensual desire for sights, sounds, smells, tastes, and touches are all different.

This is called the diversity of sensual pleasures.

And what is the result of sensual pleasures?

When one who desires sensual pleasures creates a corresponding life-form, with the attributes of either good or bad deeds—this is called the result of sensual pleasures.

And what is the cessation of sensual pleasures?

When contact ceases, sensual pleasures cease.

The practice that leads to the cessation of sensual pleasures is simply this noble eightfold path, that is:

right view, right thought, right speech, right action, right livelihood, right effort, right mindfulness, and right immersion.

When a noble disciple understands sensual pleasures in this way—and understands their source, diversity, result, cessation, and the practice that leads to their cessation—they understand that this penetrative spiritual life is the cessation of sensual pleasures.

'Sensual pleasures should be known. And their source, diversity, result, cessation, and the practice that leads to their cessation should be known.'

That's what I said, and this is why I said it.

'Feelings should be known. And their source, diversity, result, cessation, and the practice that leads to their cessation should be known.'

That's what I said, but why did I say it?

There are these three feelings:

pleasant, painful, and neutral.

And what is the source of feelings?

Contact is their source.

And what is the diversity of feelings?

There are material pleasant feelings, spiritual pleasant feelings, material painful feelings, spiritual painful feelings, material neutral feelings, and spiritual neutral feelings.

This is called the diversity of feelings.

And what is the result of feelings?

When one who feels creates a corresponding life-form, with the attributes of either good or bad deeds—

this is called the result of feelings.

And what is the cessation of feelings?

When contact ceases, feelings cease.

The practice that leads to the cessation of feelings is simply this noble eightfold path, that is:

right view, right thought, right speech, right action, right livelihood, right effort, right mindfulness, and right immersion.

When a noble disciple understands feelings in this way … they understand that this penetrative spiritual life is the cessation of feelings.

'Feelings should be known. And their source, diversity, result, cessation, and the practice that leads to their cessation should be known.'

That's what I said, and this is why I said it.

'Perceptions should be known. And their source, diversity, result, cessation, and the practice that leads to their cessation should be known.'

That's what I said, but why did I say it?

There are these six perceptions:

perceptions of sights, sounds, smells, tastes, touches, and thoughts.

And what is the source of perceptions?

Contact is their source.

And what is the diversity of perceptions?

The perceptions of sights, sounds, smells, tastes, touches, and thoughts are all different.

This is called the diversity of perceptions.

And what is the result of perceptions?

Communication is the result of perception, I say.

You communicate something in whatever manner you perceive it, saying 'That's what I perceived.'

This is called the result of perceptions.

And what is the cessation of perception?

When contact ceases, perception ceases.

The practice that leads to the cessation of perceptions is simply this noble eightfold path, that is:

right view, right thought, right speech, right action, right livelihood, right effort, right mindfulness, and right immersion.

When a noble disciple understands perception in this way … they understand that this penetrative spiritual life is the cessation of perception.

'Perceptions should be known. And their source, diversity, result, cessation, and the practice that leads to their cessation should be known.'

That's what I said, and this is why I said it.

'Defilements should be known. And their source, diversity, result, cessation, and the practice that leads to their cessation should be known.'

That's what I said, but why did I say it?

There are these three defilements:

the defilements of sensuality, desire to be reborn, and ignorance.

And what is the source of defilements?

Ignorance is the source of defilements.

And what is the diversity of defilements?

There are defilements that lead to rebirth in hell, the animal realm, the ghost realm, the human world, and the world of the gods.

This is called the diversity of defilements.

And what is the result of defilements?

When one who is ignorant creates a corresponding life-form, with the attributes of either good or bad deeds—this is called the result of defilements.

And what is the cessation of defilements?

When ignorance ceases, defilements cease.

The practice that leads to the cessation of defilements is simply this noble eightfold path, that is:

right view, right thought, right speech, right action, right livelihood, right effort, right mindfulness, and right immersion.

When a noble disciple understands defilements in this way … they understand that this penetrative spiritual life is the cessation of defilements.

'Defilements should be known. And their source, diversity, result, cessation, and the practice that leads to their cessation should be known.'

That's what I said, and this is why I said it.

'Deeds should be known. And their source, diversity, result, cessation, and the practice that leads to their cessation should be known.' That's what I said,

but why did I say it?

It is intention that I call deeds.

For after making a choice one acts

by way of body, speech, and mind.

And what is the source of deeds?

Contact is their source.

And what is the diversity of deeds?

There are deeds that lead to rebirth in hell, the animal realm, the ghost realm, the human world, and the world of the gods.

This is called the diversity of deeds.

And what is the result of deeds?

The result of deeds is threefold, I say:

in this very life, on rebirth in the next life, or at some later time.

This is called the result of deeds.

And what is the cessation of deeds?

When contact ceases, deeds cease.

The practice that leads to the cessation of deeds is simply this noble eightfold path, that is:

right view, right thought, right speech, right action, right livelihood, right effort, right mindfulness, and right immersion.

When a noble disciple understands deeds in this way … they understand that this penetrative spiritual life is the cessation of deeds.

'Deeds should be known. And their source, diversity, result, cessation, and the practice that leads to their cessation should be known.'

That's what I said, and this is why I said it.

'Suffering should be known. And its source, diversity, result, cessation, and the practice that leads to its cessation should be known.'

That's what I said, but why did I say it?

Rebirth is suffering; old age is suffering; illness is suffering; death is suffering; sorrow, lamentation, pain, sadness, and distress are suffering; not getting what you wish for is suffering. In brief, the five grasping aggregates are suffering.

And what is the source of suffering?

Craving is the source of suffering.

And what is the diversity of suffering?

There is suffering that is severe, mild, slow to fade, and quick to fade.

This is called the diversity of suffering.

And what is the result of suffering?

It's when someone who is overcome and overwhelmed by suffering sorrows and wails and laments, beating their breast and falling into confusion. Or else, overcome by that suffering, they begin an external search, wondering:

'Who knows one or two phrases to stop this suffering?'

The result of suffering is either confusion or a search, I say.

This is called the result of suffering.

And what is the cessation of suffering?

When craving ceases, suffering ceases.

The practice that leads to the cessation of suffering is simply this noble eightfold path, that is:

right view, right thought, right speech, right action, right livelihood, right effort, right mindfulness, and right immersion.

When a noble disciple understands suffering in this way … they understand that this penetrative spiritual life is the cessation of suffering.

'Suffering should be known. And its source, diversity, result, cessation, and the practice that leads to its cessation should be known.'

That's what I said, and this is why I said it.

This is the penetrative exposition of the teaching."

SAMADHIPARIKKHARASUTTA:

Prerequisites for Immersion

"Mendicants, there are these seven prerequisites for immersion.

What seven?

Right view, right thought, right speech, right action, right livelihood, right effort, and right mindfulness.

Unification of mind with these seven factors as prerequisites is called noble right immersion 'with its vital conditions' and 'with its prerequisites'."

MICCHATTASUTTA:

The Wrong Way

"Mendicants, relying on the wrong way leads to failure, not success.

And how does relying on the wrong way lead to failure, not success?

Wrong view gives rise to wrong thought. Wrong thought gives rise to wrong speech. Wrong speech gives rise to wrong action. Wrong action gives rise to wrong livelihood. Wrong livelihood gives rise to wrong effort. Wrong effort gives rise to wrong mindfulness. Wrong mindfulness gives rise to wrong immersion. Wrong immersion gives rise to wrong knowledge. Wrong knowledge gives rise to wrong freedom.

That's how relying on the wrong way leads to failure, not success.

Relying on the right way leads to success, not failure.

And how does relying on the right way lead to success, not failure?

Right view gives rise to right thought. Right thought gives rise to right speech. Right speech gives rise to right action. Right action gives rise to right livelihood. Right livelihood gives rise to right effort. Right effort gives rise to right mindfulness. Right mindfulness gives rise to right immersion. Right immersion gives rise to right knowledge. Right knowledge gives rise to right freedom.

That's how relying on the right way leads to success, not failure."

VIJJASUTTA:

Knowledge

"Mendicants, ignorance precedes the attainment of unskillful qualities, with lack of conscience and prudence following along.

An ignoramus, sunk in ignorance, gives rise to wrong view. Wrong view gives rise to wrong thought. Wrong thought gives rise to wrong speech. Wrong speech gives rise to wrong action. Wrong action gives rise to wrong livelihood. Wrong livelihood gives rise to wrong effort. Wrong effort gives rise to wrong mindfulness. Wrong mindfulness gives rise to wrong immersion. Wrong immersion gives rise to wrong knowledge. Wrong knowledge gives rise to wrong freedom.

Knowledge precedes the attainment of skillful qualities, with conscience and prudence following along.

A sage, firm in knowledge, gives rise to right view. Right view gives rise to right thought. Right thought gives rise to right speech. Right speech gives rise to right action. Right action gives rise to right livelihood. Right livelihood gives rise to right effort. Right effort gives rise to right mindfulness. Right mindfulness gives rise to right immersion. Right immersion gives rise to right knowledge. Right knowledge gives rise to right freedom."

Nijjarasutta:

Wearing Away

"Mendicants, there are these ten grounds for wearing away.

What ten?

For one of right view, wrong view is worn away.

And the many bad, unskillful qualities that arise because of wrong view are worn away.

And because of right view, many skillful qualities are fully developed.

For one of right thought, wrong thought is worn away.

And the many bad, unskillful qualities that arise because of wrong thought are worn away.

And because of right thought, many skillful qualities are fully developed.

For one of right speech, wrong speech is worn away.

And the many bad, unskillful qualities that arise because of wrong speech are worn away.

And because of right speech, many skillful qualities are fully developed.

For one of right action, wrong action is worn away.

And the many bad, unskillful qualities that arise because of wrong action are worn away.

And because of right action, many skillful qualities are fully developed.

For one of right livelihood, wrong livelihood is worn away.

And the many bad, unskillful qualities that arise because of wrong livelihood are worn away.

And because of right livelihood, many skillful qualities are fully developed.

For one of right effort, wrong effort is worn away.

And the many bad, unskillful qualities that arise because of wrong effort are worn away.

And because of right effort, many skillful qualities are fully developed.

For one of right mindfulness, wrong mindfulness is worn away.

And the many bad, unskillful qualities that arise because of wrong mindfulness are worn away.

And because of right mindfulness, many skillful qualities are fully developed.

For one of right immersion, wrong immersion is worn away.

And the many bad, unskillful qualities that arise because of wrong immersion are worn away.

And because of right immersion, many skillful qualities are fully developed.

For one of right knowledge, wrong knowledge is worn away.

And the many bad, unskillful qualities that arise because of wrong knowledge are worn away.

And because of right knowledge, many skillful qualities are fully developed.

For one of right freedom, wrong freedom is worn away.

And the many bad, unskillful qualities that arise because of wrong freedom are worn away.

And because of right freedom, many skillful qualities are fully developed.

These are the ten grounds for wearing away."

DHOVANASUTTA:

Washing

"Mendicants, there is a country in the south called 'Washing'.

They have food, drink, snacks, meals, refreshments, and beverages, as well as dancing, singing, and music.

There is such a 'Washing', I don't deny it.

But that washing is low, crude, ordinary, ignoble, and pointless. It doesn't lead to disillusionment, dispassion, cessation, peace, insight, awakening, and extinguishment.

I will teach a noble washing that leads solely to disillusionment, dispassion, cessation, peace, insight, awakening, and extinguishment. Relying on that washing, sentient beings who are liable to rebirth, old age, and death, to sorrow, lamentation, pain, sadness, and distress are freed from all these things.

Listen and pay close attention, I will speak."

"Yes, sir," they replied.

The Buddha said this:

"And what is that noble washing?

For one of right view, wrong view is washed away.

And the many bad, unskillful qualities that arise because of wrong view are washed away.

And because of right view, many skillful qualities are fully developed.

For one of right thought, wrong thought is washed away. …

For one of right speech, wrong speech is washed away. …

For one of right action, wrong action is washed away. …

For one of right livelihood, wrong livelihood is washed away. …

For one of right effort, wrong effort is washed away. …

For one of right mindfulness, wrong mindfulness is washed away. …

For one of right immersion, wrong immersion is washed away. …

For one of right knowledge, wrong knowledge is washed away. …

For one of right freedom, wrong freedom is washed away.

And the many bad, unskillful qualities that arise because of wrong freedom are washed away.

And because of right freedom, many skillful qualities are fully developed.

This is the noble washing that leads solely to disillusionment, dispassion, cessation, peace, insight, awakening, and extinguishment. Relying on this washing, sentient beings who are liable to rebirth, old age, and death, to sorrow, lamentation, pain, sadness, and distress are freed from all these things."

TIKICCHAKASUTTA:

Doctors

"Mendicants, doctors prescribe a purgative for eliminating illnesses stemming from disorders of bile, phlegm, and wind.

There is such a purgative, I don't deny it.

But this kind of purgative sometimes works and sometimes fails.

I will teach a noble purgative that works without fail. Relying on that purgative, sentient beings who are liable to rebirth, old age, and death, to sorrow, lamentation, pain, sadness, and distress are freed from all these things.

Listen and pay close attention, I will speak."

"Yes, sir," they replied.

The Buddha said this:

"And what is the noble purgative that works without fail?

For one of right view, wrong view is purged.

And the many bad, unskillful qualities produced by wrong view are purged.

And because of right view, many skillful qualities are fully developed.

For one of right thought, wrong thought is purged. …

For one of right speech, wrong speech is purged. …

For one of right action, wrong action is purged. …

For one of right livelihood, wrong livelihood is purged. …

For one of right effort, wrong effort is purged.

For one of right mindfulness, wrong mindfulness is purged. …

For one of right immersion, wrong immersion is purged. …

For one of right knowledge, wrong knowledge is purged. …

For one of right freedom, wrong freedom is purged.

And the many bad, unskillful qualities produced by wrong freedom are purged.

And because of right freedom, many skillful qualities are fully developed.

This is the noble purgative that works without fail. Relying on this purgative, sentient beings who are liable to rebirth, old age, and death, to sorrow, lamentation, pain, sadness, and distress are freed from all these things."

VAMANASUTTA:

Emetic

"Mendicants, doctors prescribe an emetic for eliminating illnesses stemming from disorders of bile, phlegm, and wind.

There is such an emetic, I don't deny it.

But this kind of emetic sometimes works and sometimes fails.

I will teach a noble emetic that works without fail. Relying on that emetic, sentient beings who are liable to rebirth, old age, and death, to sorrow, lamentation, pain, sadness, and distress are freed from all these things.

Listen and pay close attention, I will speak. …

And what is that noble emetic that works without fail?

For one of right view, wrong view is vomited up.

And the many bad, unskillful qualities produced by wrong view are vomited up.

And because of right view, many skillful qualities are fully developed.

For one of right thought, wrong thought is vomited up. …

For one of right speech, wrong speech is vomited up. …

For one of right action, wrong action is vomited up. …

For one of right livelihood, wrong livelihood is vomited up. …

For one of right effort, wrong effort is vomited up. …

For one of right mindfulness, wrong mindfulness is vomited up. …

For one of right immersion, wrong immersion is vomited up. …

For one of right knowledge, wrong knowledge is vomited up. …

For one of right freedom, wrong freedom is vomited up.

And the many bad, unskillful qualities produced by wrong freedom are vomited up.

And because of right freedom, many skillful qualities are fully developed.

This is the noble emetic that works without fail. Relying on this emetic, sentient beings who are liable to rebirth, old age, and death, to sorrow, lamentation, pain, sadness, and distress are freed from all these things."

NIDDHAMANĪYASUTTA:

Blown Away

"Mendicants, these ten qualities should be blown away.

What ten?

For one of right view, wrong view is blown away.

And the many bad, unskillful qualities produced by wrong view are blown away.

And because of right view, many skillful qualities are fully developed.

For one of right thought, wrong thought is blown away. …

For one of right speech, wrong speech is blown away. …

For one of right action, wrong action is blown away. …

For one of right livelihood, wrong livelihood is blown away. …

For one of right effort, wrong effort is blown away. …

For one of right mindfulness, wrong mindfulness is blown away. …

For one of right immersion, wrong immersion is blown away. …

For one of right knowledge, wrong knowledge is blown away. …

For one of right freedom, wrong freedom is blown away.

And the many bad, unskillful qualities produced by wrong freedom are blown away.

And because of right freedom, many skillful qualities are fully developed.

These are the ten qualities that should be blown away."

Pathamaasekhasutta:

An Adept (1st)

Then a mendicant went up to the Buddha, bowed, sat down to one side, and said to him:

"Sir, they speak of this person called 'an adept'.

How is an adept mendicant defined?"

"Mendicant, it's when a mendicant has an adept's right view, right thought, right speech, right action, right livelihood, right effort, right mindfulness, right immersion, right knowledge, and right freedom.

That's how a mendicant is an adept."

Dutiyaasekhasutta:

An Adept (2nd)

"Mendicants, there are ten qualities of an adept.

What ten?

An adept's right view, right thought, right speech, right action, right livelihood, right effort, right mindfulness, right immersion, right knowledge, and right freedom.

These are the ten qualities of an adept."

PATHAMAADHAMMASUTTA:

Bad Principles (1st)

"Mendicants, you should know bad principles with bad results.

And you should know good principles with good results.

Knowing these things, your practice should follow the good principles with good results.

And what are bad principles with bad results?

Wrong view, wrong thought, wrong speech, wrong action, wrong livelihood, wrong effort, wrong mindfulness, wrong immersion, wrong knowledge, and wrong freedom.

These are called bad principles with bad results.

And what are good principles with good results?

Right view, right thought, right speech, right action, right livelihood, right effort, right mindfulness, right immersion, right knowledge, and right freedom.

These are called good principles with good results.

'You should know bad principles with bad results.

And you should know good principles with good results.

Knowing these things, your practice should follow the good principles with good results.'

That's what I said, and this is why I said it."

DUTIYAADHAMMASUTTA:

Bad Principles (2nd)

"Mendicants, you should know bad principles and good principles.

And you should know bad results and good results.

Knowing these things, your practice should follow the good principles with good results.

So what are bad principles? What are good principles? What are bad results? And what are good results?

Wrong view is a bad principle.

Right view is a good principle.

And the many bad, unskillful qualities produced by wrong view are bad results.

And the many skillful qualities fully developed because of right view are good results.

Wrong thought is a bad principle.

Right thought is a good principle.

And the many bad, unskillful qualities produced by wrong thought are bad results.

And the many skillful qualities fully developed because of right thought are good results.

Wrong speech is a bad principle.

Right speech is a good principle.

And the many bad, unskillful qualities produced by wrong speech are bad results.

And the many skillful qualities fully developed because of right speech are good results.

Wrong action is a bad principle.

Right action is a good principle.

And the many bad, unskillful qualities produced by wrong action are bad results.

And the many skillful qualities fully developed because of right action are good results.

Wrong livelihood is a bad principle.

Right livelihood is a good principle.

And the many bad, unskillful qualities produced by wrong livelihood are bad results.

And the many skillful qualities fully developed because of right livelihood are good results.

Wrong effort is a bad principle.

Right effort is a good principle.

And the many bad, unskillful qualities produced by wrong effort are bad results.

And the many skillful qualities fully developed because of right effort are good results.

Wrong mindfulness is a bad principle.

Right mindfulness is a good principle.

And the many bad, unskillful qualities produced by wrong mindfulness are bad results.

And the many skillful qualities fully developed because of right mindfulness are good results.

Wrong immersion is a bad principle.

Right immersion is a good principle.

And the many bad, unskillful qualities produced by wrong immersion are bad results.

And the many skillful qualities fully developed because of right immersion are good results.

Wrong knowledge is a bad principle.

Right knowledge is a good principle.

And the many bad, unskillful qualities produced by wrong knowledge are bad results.

And the many skillful qualities fully developed because of right knowledge are good results.

Wrong freedom is a bad principle.

Right freedom is a good principle.

And the many bad, unskillful qualities produced by wrong freedom are bad results.

And the many skillful qualities fully developed because of right freedom are good results.

'You should know bad principles and good principles.

And you should know bad results and good results.

Knowing these things, your practice should follow the good principles with good results.'

That's what I said, and this is why I said it."

TATIYAADHAMMASUTTA:

Bad Principles (3rd)

"Mendicants, you should know bad principles and good principles.

And you should know bad results and good results.

Knowing these things, your practice should follow the good principles with good results."

That is what the Buddha said.

When he had spoken, the Holy One got up from his seat and entered his dwelling.

Soon after the Buddha left, those mendicants considered,

"The Buddha gave this brief passage for recitation, then entered his dwelling without explaining the meaning in detail.

Who can explain in detail the meaning of this brief passage for recitation given by the Buddha?"

Then they considered,

"This Venerable Ananda is praised by the Buddha and esteemed by his sensible spiritual companions.

He is capable of explaining in detail the meaning of this brief passage for recitation given by the Buddha.

Let's go to him, and ask him about this matter.

As he answers, so we'll remember it."

Then those mendicants went to Ananda, and exchanged greetings with him.

When the greetings and polite conversation were over, they sat down to one side. They told him what had happened, and said,

"May Venerable Ananda please explain this."

"Reverends, suppose there was a person in need of heartwood. And while wandering in search of heartwood he'd come across a large tree standing with heartwood. But he'd pass over the roots and trunk, imagining that the heartwood should be sought in the branches and leaves.

Such is the consequence for the venerables. Though you were face to face with the Buddha, you overlooked him, imagining that you should ask me about this matter.

For he is the Buddha, who knows and sees. He is vision, he is knowledge, he is the truth, he is holiness. He is the teacher, the proclaimer, the elucidator of meaning, the bestower of the deathless, the lord of truth, the Realized One.

That was the time to approach the Buddha and ask about this matter.

You should have remembered it in line with the Buddha's answer."

"Certainly he is the Buddha, who knows and sees. He is vision, he is knowledge, he is the truth, he is holiness. He is the teacher, the proclaimer, the elucidator of meaning, the bestower of the deathless, the lord of truth, the Realized One.

That was the time to approach the Buddha and ask about this matter.

We should have remembered it in line with the Buddha's answer.

Still, Venerable Ananda is praised by the Buddha and esteemed by his sensible spiritual companions.

You are capable of explaining in detail the meaning of this brief passage for recitation given by the Buddha.

Please explain this, if it's no trouble."

"Then listen and pay close attention, I will speak."

"Yes, reverend," they replied.

Ananda said this:

"Reverends, the Buddha gave this brief passage for recitation, then entered his dwelling without explaining the meaning in detail:

'You should know bad principles and good principles.

And you should know bad results and good results.

Knowing these things, your practice should follow the good principles with good results.'

So what are bad principles? What are good principles? What are bad results? And what are good results?

Wrong view is a bad principle.

Right view is a good principle.

And the many bad, unskillful qualities produced by wrong view are bad results.

And the many skillful qualities fully developed because of right view are good results.

Wrong thought is a bad principle.

Right thought is a good principle. …

Wrong speech is a bad principle.

Right speech is a good principle. …

Wrong action is a bad principle.

Right action is a good principle. …

Wrong livelihood is a bad principle.

Right livelihood is a good principle. …

Wrong effort is a bad principle.

Right effort is a good principle. …

Wrong mindfulness is a bad principle.

Right mindfulness is a good principle. …

Wrong immersion is a bad principle.

Right immersion is a good principle. …

Wrong knowledge is a bad principle.

Right knowledge is a good principle. …

Wrong freedom is a bad principle.

Right freedom is a good principle.

And the many bad, unskillful qualities produced by wrong freedom are bad results.

And the many skillful qualities fully developed because of right freedom are good results.

The Buddha gave this brief passage for recitation, then entered his dwelling without explaining the meaning in detail:

'You should know bad principles and good principles …

and practice accordingly.' And this is how I understand the detailed meaning of this passage for recitation.

If you wish, you may go to the Buddha and ask him about this.

You should remember it in line with the Buddha's answer."

"Yes, reverend," said those mendicants, approving and agreeing with what Ananda said. Then they rose from their seats and went to the Buddha, bowed, sat down to one side, and told him what had happened. Then they said:

"Sir, we went to Ananda and asked him about this matter.

And Ananda clearly explained the meaning to us in this manner, with these words and phrases."

"Good, good, mendicants!

Ananda is astute,

he has great wisdom.

If you came to me and asked this question, I would answer it in exactly the same way as Ananda.

That is what it means, and that's how you should remember it."

AJITASUTTA:

With Ajita

Then the wanderer Ajita went up to the Buddha, and exchanged greetings with him.

When the greetings and polite conversation were over, he sat down to one side and said to the Buddha,

"Master Gotama, we have a spiritual companion called 'The Philosopher'.

He has worked out around five hundred arguments by which followers of other religions will know when they've been refuted."

Then the Buddha said to the mendicants,

"Mendicants, do you remember this philosopher's points?"

"Now is the time, Blessed One! Now is the time, Holy One!

Let the Buddha speak and the mendicants will remember it."

"Well then, mendicants, listen and pay close attention, I will speak."

"Yes, sir," they replied.

The Buddha said this:

"Mendicants, take a certain person who rebuts and quashes unprincipled statements with unprincipled statements. This delights an unprincipled assembly,

who make a dreadful racket:

'He's a true philosopher! He's a true philosopher!'

Another person rebuts and quashes principled statements with unprincipled statements. This delights an unprincipled assembly,

who make a dreadful racket:

'He's a true philosopher! He's a true philosopher!'

Another person rebuts and quashes principled and unprincipled statements with unprincipled statements. This delights an unprincipled assembly,

who make a dreadful racket:

'He's a true philosopher! He's a true philosopher!'

Mendicants, you should know bad principles and good principles.

And you should know bad results and good results.

Knowing these things, your practice should follow the good principles with good results.

So what are bad principles? What are good principles? What are bad results? And what are good results?

Wrong view is a bad principle.

Right view is a good principle.

And the many bad, unskillful qualities produced by wrong view are bad results.

And the many skillful qualities fully developed because of right view are good results.

Wrong thought is a bad principle.

Right thought is a good principle. …

Wrong speech is a bad principle.

Right speech is a good principle. …

Wrong action is a bad principle.

Right action is a good principle. …

Wrong livelihood is a bad principle.

Right livelihood is a good principle. …

Wrong effort is a bad principle.

Right effort is a good principle. …

Wrong mindfulness is a bad principle.

Right mindfulness is a good principle. …

Wrong immersion is a bad principle.

Right immersion is a good principle. …

Wrong knowledge is a bad principle.

Right knowledge is a good principle. …

Wrong freedom is a bad principle.

Right freedom is a good principle.

And the many bad, unskillful qualities produced by wrong freedom are bad results.

And the many skillful qualities fully developed because of right freedom are good results.

'You should know bad principles and good principles.

And you should know bad results and good results.

Knowing these things, your practice should follow the good principles with good results.'

That's what I said, and this is why I said it."

SAṄGARAVASUTTA:

With Saṅgarava

Then Saṅgarava the brahmin went up to the Buddha, and exchanged greetings with him.

When the greetings and polite conversation were over, he sat down to one side and said to the Buddha:

"Master Gotama, what is the near shore? And what is the far shore?"

"Wrong view is the near shore, brahmin, and right view is the far shore.

Wrong thought is the near shore, and right thought is the far shore.

Wrong speech is the near shore, and right speech is the far shore.

Wrong action is the near shore, and right action is the far shore.

Wrong livelihood is the near shore, and right livelihood is the far shore.

Wrong effort is the near shore, and right effort is the far shore.

Wrong mindfulness is the near shore, and right mindfulness is the far shore.

Wrong immersion is the near shore, and right immersion is the far shore.

Wrong knowledge is the near shore, and right knowledge is the far shore.

Wrong freedom is the near shore, and right freedom is the far shore.

This is the near shore, and this is the far shore.

Few are those among humans

who cross to the far shore.

The rest just run around

on the near shore.

When the teaching is well explained,

those who practice accordingly

are the ones who will cross over

Death's domain so hard to pass.

Rid of dark qualities,

an astute person should develop the bright.

Leaving home behind

for the seclusion so hard to enjoy,

find delight there,

having left behind sensual pleasures.

With no possessions, an astute person

would cleanse themselves of mental corruptions.

Those whose minds are rightly developed

in the awakening factors;

who, letting go of attachments,

delight in not grasping:

with defilements ended, brilliant,

they in this world are quenched."

PUBBAṄGAMASUTTA:

Forerunner

"Mendicants, the dawn is the forerunner and precursor of the sunrise.

In the same way right view is the forerunner and precursor of skillful qualities.

Right view gives rise to right thought. Right thought gives rise to right speech. Right speech gives rise to right action. Right action gives rise to right livelihood. Right livelihood gives rise to right effort. Right effort gives rise to right mindfulness. Right mindfulness gives rise to right immersion. Right immersion gives rise to right knowledge. Right knowledge gives rise to right freedom."

ASAVAKKHAYASUTTA:

The Ending of Defilements

"Mendicants, these ten things, when developed and cultivated, lead to the ending of defilements.

What ten?

Right view, right thought, right speech, right action, right livelihood, right effort, right mindfulness, right immersion, right knowledge, and right freedom.

These ten things, when developed and cultivated, lead to the ending of defilements."

PATHAMASUTTA:

First

"Mendicants, these ten things are not purified and cleansed apart from the Holy One's training.

What ten?

Right view, right thought, right speech, right action, right livelihood, right effort, right mindfulness, right immersion, right knowledge, and right freedom.

These ten things are not purified and cleansed apart from the Holy One's training."

DUTIYASUTTA:

Second

"Mendicants, these ten things don't arise apart from the Holy One's training.

What ten?

Right view, right thought, right speech, right action, right livelihood, right effort, right mindfulness, right immersion, right knowledge, and right freedom.

These are the ten things that don't arise apart from the Holy One's training."

TATIYASUTTA:

Third

"Mendicants, these ten things are not very fruitful and beneficial apart from the Holy One's training.

What ten?

Right view, right thought, right speech, right action, right livelihood, right effort, right mindfulness, right immersion, right knowledge, and right freedom.

These are the ten things that are not very fruitful and beneficial apart from the Holy One's training."

CATUTTHASUTTA:

Fourth

"Mendicants, these ten things don't culminate in the removal of greed, hate, and delusion apart from the Holy One's training.

What ten?

Right view, right thought, right speech, right action, right livelihood, right effort, right mindfulness, right immersion, right knowledge, and right freedom.

These are the ten things that don't culminate in the removal of greed, hate, and delusion apart from the Holy One's training."

PAÑCAMASUTTA:

Fifth

"Mendicants, these ten things don't lead solely to disillusionment, dispassion, cessation, peace, insight, awakening, and extinguishment apart from the Holy One's training.

What ten?

Right view, right thought, right speech, right action, right livelihood, right effort, right mindfulness, right immersion, right knowledge, and right freedom.

These are the ten things that don't lead solely to disillusionment, dispassion, cessation, peace, insight, awakening, and extinguishment apart from the Holy One's training."

CHATTHASUTTA:

Sixth

"Mendicants, these ten things don't arise to be developed and cultivated apart from the Holy One's training.

What ten?

Right view, right thought, right speech, right action, right livelihood, right effort, right mindfulness, right immersion, right knowledge, and right freedom.

These are the ten things that don't arise to be developed and cultivated apart from the Holy One's training."

SATTAMASUTTA:

Seventh

"Mendicants, these ten things when developed and cultivated are not very fruitful and beneficial apart from the Holy One's training.

What ten?

Right view, right thought, right speech, right action, right livelihood, right effort, right mindfulness, right immersion, right knowledge, and right freedom.

These are the ten things that when developed and cultivated are not very fruitful and beneficial apart from the Holy One's training."

ATTHAMASUTTA:

Eighth

"Mendicants, these ten things when developed and cultivated don't culminate in the removal of greed, hate, and delusion apart from the Holy One's training.

What ten?

Right view, right thought, right speech, right action, right livelihood, right effort, right mindfulness, right immersion, right knowledge, and right freedom.

These are the ten things that when developed and cultivated don't culminate in the removal of greed, hate, and delusion apart from the Holy One's training."

NAVAMASUTTA:

Ninth

"Mendicants, these ten things when developed and cultivated don't lead solely to disillusionment, dispassion, cessation, peace, insight, awakening, and extinguishment apart from the Holy One's training.

What ten?

Right view, right thought, right speech, right action, right livelihood, right effort, right mindfulness, right immersion, right knowledge, and right freedom.

These are the ten things that when developed and cultivated don't lead solely to disillusionment, dispassion, cessation, peace, insight, awakening, and extinguishment apart from the Holy One's training."

DASAMASUTTA:

Tenth

"Mendicants, there are ten wrong ways.

What ten?

Wrong view, wrong thought, wrong speech, wrong action, wrong livelihood, wrong effort, wrong mindfulness, wrong immersion, wrong knowledge, and wrong freedom.

These are the ten wrong ways."

EKADASAMASUTTA:

Eleventh

"Mendicants, there are ten right ways.

What ten?

Right view, right thought, right speech, right action, right livelihood, right effort, right mindfulness, right immersion, right knowledge, and right freedom.

These are the ten right ways."

SADHUSUTTA:

Good

"Mendicants, I will teach you what is good and what is not good.

Listen and pay close attention, I will speak."

"Yes, sir," they replied.

The Buddha said this:

"And what, mendicants, is not good?

Wrong view, wrong thought, wrong speech, wrong action, wrong livelihood, wrong effort, wrong mindfulness, wrong immersion, wrong knowledge, and wrong freedom.

This is called what is not good.

And what is good?

Right view, right thought, right speech, right action, right livelihood, right effort, right mindfulness, right immersion, right knowledge, and right freedom.

This is called what is good."

ARIYADHAMMASUTTA:

The Teaching of the Noble Ones

"Mendicants, I will teach you the teaching of the noble ones, and what is not the teaching of the noble ones. …

And what is not the teaching of the noble ones?

Wrong view, wrong thought, wrong speech, wrong action, wrong livelihood, wrong effort, wrong mindfulness, wrong immersion, wrong knowledge, and wrong freedom.

This is called what is not the teaching of the noble ones.

And what is the teaching of the noble ones?

Right view, right thought, right speech, right action, right livelihood, right effort, right mindfulness, right immersion, right knowledge, and right freedom.

This is called the teaching of the noble ones."

AKUSALASUTTA:

Unskillful

"I will teach you the skillful and the unskillful …

And what is the unskillful?

Wrong view, wrong thought, wrong speech, wrong action, wrong livelihood, wrong effort, wrong mindfulness, wrong immersion, wrong knowledge, and wrong freedom.

This is called the unskillful.

And what is the skillful?

Right view, right thought, right speech, right action, right livelihood, right effort, right mindfulness, right immersion, right knowledge, and right freedom.

This is called the skillful."

ATTHASUTTA:

Beneficial

"I will teach you the beneficial and the harmful. …

And what is the harmful?

Wrong view, wrong thought, wrong speech, wrong action, wrong livelihood, wrong effort, wrong mindfulness, wrong immersion, wrong knowledge, and wrong freedom.

This is called the harmful.

And what is the beneficial?

Right view, right thought, right speech, right action, right livelihood, right effort, right mindfulness, right immersion, right knowledge, and right freedom.

This is called the beneficial."

DHAMMASUTTA:

The Teaching

"I will teach you what is the teaching and what is not the teaching. …

And what is not the teaching?

Wrong view, wrong thought, wrong speech, wrong action, wrong livelihood, wrong effort, wrong mindfulness, wrong immersion, wrong knowledge, and wrong freedom.

This is called what is not the teaching.

And what is the teaching?

Right view, right thought, right speech, right action, right livelihood, right effort, right mindfulness, right immersion, right knowledge, and right freedom.

This is called the teaching."

SASAVASUTTA:

Defiled

"I will teach you the defiled principle and the undefiled. …

And what is the defiled principle?

Wrong view, wrong thought, wrong speech, wrong action, wrong livelihood, wrong effort, wrong mindfulness, wrong immersion, wrong knowledge, and wrong freedom.

This is called the defiled principle.

And what is the undefiled principle?

Right view, right thought, right speech, right action, right livelihood, right effort, right mindfulness, right immersion, right knowledge, and right freedom.

This is called the undefiled principle."

SAVAJJASUTTA:

Blameworthy

"I will teach you the blameworthy principle and the blameless principle. …

And what is the blameworthy principle?

Wrong view, wrong thought, wrong speech, wrong action, wrong livelihood, wrong effort, wrong mindfulness, wrong immersion, wrong knowledge, and wrong freedom.

This is called the blameworthy principle.

And what is the blameless principle?

Right view, right thought, right speech, right action, right livelihood, right effort, right mindfulness, right immersion, right knowledge, and right freedom.

This is called the blameless principle."

TAPANĪYASUTTA:

Mortifying

"I will teach you the mortifying principle and the unmortifying. …

And what is the mortifying principle?

Wrong view, wrong thought, wrong speech, wrong action, wrong livelihood, wrong effort, wrong mindfulness, wrong immersion, wrong knowledge, and wrong freedom.

This is called the mortifying principle.

And what is the unmortifying principle?

Right view, right thought, right speech, right action, right livelihood, right effort, right mindfulness, right immersion, right knowledge, and right freedom.

This is called the unmortifying principle."

ACAYAGAMISUTTA:

Accumulation

"I will teach you the principle that leads to accumulation and that which leads to dispersal. …

And what is the principle that leads to accumulation?

Wrong view, wrong thought, wrong speech, wrong action, wrong livelihood, wrong effort, wrong mindfulness, wrong immersion, wrong knowledge, and wrong freedom.

This is called the principle that leads to accumulation.

And what is the principle that leads to dispersal?

Right view, right thought, right speech, right action, right livelihood, right effort, right mindfulness, right immersion, right knowledge, and right freedom.

This is called the principle that leads to dispersal."

DUKKHUDRAYASUTTA:

With Suffering as Outcome

"I will teach you the principle that has suffering as outcome, and that which has happiness as outcome. …

And what is the principle whose outcome is suffering?

Wrong view, wrong thought, wrong speech, wrong action, wrong livelihood, wrong effort, wrong mindfulness, wrong immersion, wrong knowledge, and wrong freedom.

This is the principle whose outcome is suffering.

And what is the principle whose outcome is happiness?

Right view, right thought, right speech, right action, right livelihood, right effort, right mindfulness, right immersion, right knowledge, and right freedom.

This is the principle whose outcome is happiness."

DUKKHAVIPAKASUTTA:

Result in Suffering

"I will teach you the principle that results in suffering and that which results in happiness. …

And what principle results in suffering?

Wrong view, wrong thought, wrong speech, wrong action, wrong livelihood, wrong effort, wrong mindfulness, wrong immersion, wrong knowledge, and wrong freedom.

This is called the principle that results in suffering.

And what principle results in happiness?

Right view, right thought, right speech, right action, right livelihood, right effort, right mindfulness, right immersion, right knowledge, and right freedom.

This is called the principle that results in happiness."

ARIYAMAGGASUTTA:

The Noble Path

"I will teach you the noble path and the ignoble path. ...

And what is the ignoble path?

Wrong view, wrong thought, wrong speech, wrong action, wrong livelihood, wrong effort, wrong mindfulness, wrong immersion, wrong knowledge, and wrong freedom.

This is called the ignoble path.

And what is the noble path?

Right view, right thought, right speech, right action, right livelihood, right effort, right mindfulness, right immersion, right knowledge, and right freedom.

This is called the noble path."

KANHAMAGGASUTTA:

The Dark Path

"I will teach you the dark path and the bright path. ...

And what is the dark path?

Wrong view, wrong thought, wrong speech, wrong action, wrong livelihood, wrong effort, wrong mindfulness, wrong immersion, wrong knowledge, and wrong freedom.

This is called the dark path.

And what is the bright path?

Right view, right thought, right speech, right action, right livelihood, right effort, right mindfulness, right immersion, right knowledge, and right freedom.

This is called the bright path."

SADDHAMMASUTTA:

The True Teaching

"I will teach you what is the true teaching and what is not the true teaching. …

And what is not the true teaching?

Wrong view, wrong thought, wrong speech, wrong action, wrong livelihood, wrong effort, wrong mindfulness, wrong immersion, wrong knowledge, and wrong freedom.

This is called what is not the true teaching.

And what is the true teaching?

Right view, right thought, right speech, right action, right livelihood, right effort, right mindfulness, right immersion, right knowledge, and right freedom.

This is called the true teaching."

SAPPURISADHAMMASUTTA:

The Teaching of the Good Persons

"Mendicants, I will teach you the teaching of the good persons and the teaching of the bad persons. …

And what is the teaching of the bad persons?

Wrong view, wrong thought, wrong speech, wrong action, wrong livelihood, wrong effort, wrong mindfulness, wrong immersion, wrong knowledge, and wrong freedom.

This is the teaching of the bad persons.

And what is the teaching of the good persons?

Right view, right thought, right speech, right action, right livelihood, right effort, right mindfulness, right immersion, right knowledge, and right freedom.

This is the teaching of the good persons."

UPPADETABBASUTTA:

Should Be Activated

"I will teach you the principle to activate and the principle not to activate. …

And what is the principle not to activate?

Wrong view, wrong thought, wrong speech, wrong action, wrong livelihood, wrong effort, wrong mindfulness, wrong immersion, wrong knowledge, and wrong freedom.

This is called the principle not to activate.

And what is the principle to activate?

Right view, right thought, right speech, right action, right livelihood, right effort, right mindfulness, right immersion, right knowledge, and right freedom.

This is called the principle to activate."

ASEVITABBASUTTA:

Should Be Cultivated

"I will teach you the principle to cultivate and the principle not to cultivate. …

And what is the principle not to cultivate?

Wrong view, wrong thought, wrong speech, wrong action, wrong livelihood, wrong effort, wrong mindfulness, wrong immersion, wrong knowledge, and wrong freedom.

This is called the principle not to cultivate.

And what is the principle to cultivate?

Right view, right thought, right speech, right action, right livelihood, right effort, right mindfulness, right immersion, right knowledge, and right freedom.

This is called the principle to cultivate."

BHAVETABBASUTTA:

Should Be Developed

"I will teach you the principle to develop and the principle not to develop. …

And what is the principle not to develop?

Wrong view, wrong thought, wrong speech, wrong action, wrong livelihood, wrong effort, wrong mindfulness, wrong immersion, wrong knowledge, and wrong freedom.

This is called the principle not to develop.

And what is the principle to develop?

Right view, right thought, right speech, right action, right livelihood, right effort, right mindfulness, right immersion, right knowledge, and right freedom.

This is called the principle to develop."

BAHULĪKATABBASUTTA:

Should Be Made Much Of

"I will teach you the principle to make much of and the principle not to make much of. …

And what is the principle not to make much of?

Wrong view, wrong thought, wrong speech, wrong action, wrong livelihood, wrong effort, wrong mindfulness, wrong immersion, wrong knowledge, and wrong freedom.

This is called the principle not to make much of.

And what is the principle to make much of?

Right view, right thought, right speech, right action, right livelihood, right effort, right mindfulness, right immersion, right knowledge, and right freedom.

This is called the principle to make much of."

ANUSSARITABBASUTTA:

Should Be Recollected

"I will teach you the principle to recollect and the principle not to recollect. …

And what is the principle not to recollect?

Wrong view, wrong thought, wrong speech, wrong action, wrong livelihood, wrong effort, wrong mindfulness, wrong immersion, wrong knowledge, and wrong freedom.

This is called the principle not to recollect.

And what is the principle to recollect?

Right view, right thought, right speech, right action, right livelihood, right effort, right mindfulness, right immersion, right knowledge, and right freedom.

This is called the principle to recollect."

SACCHIKATABBASUTTA:

Should Be Realized

"I will teach you the principle to realize and the principle not to realize. …

And what is the principle not to realize?

Wrong view, wrong thought, wrong speech, wrong action, wrong livelihood, wrong effort, wrong mindfulness, wrong immersion, wrong knowledge, and wrong freedom.

This is called the principle not to realize.

And what is the principle to realize?

Right view, right thought, right speech, right action, right livelihood, right effort, right mindfulness, right immersion, right knowledge, and right freedom.

This is called the principle to realize."

SEVITABBASUTTA:

You Should Associate

"Mendicants, you should not associate with a person who has ten qualities.

What ten?

Wrong view, wrong thought, wrong speech, wrong action, wrong livelihood, wrong effort, wrong mindfulness, wrong immersion, wrong knowledge, and wrong freedom.

You should not associate with a person who has these ten qualities.

You should associate with a person who has ten qualities.

What ten?

Right view, right thought, right speech, right action, right livelihood, right effort, right mindfulness, right immersion, right knowledge, and right freedom.

You should associate with a person who has these ten qualities."

BHAJITABBADISUTTA:

Frequenting, Etc.

"Mendicants, you should not frequent a person who has ten qualities. …

you should frequent …

you should not pay homage …

you should pay homage …

you should not venerate …

you should venerate …

you should not praise …

you should praise …

you should not respect …

you should respect …

you should not revere …

you should revere …

is not a success …

is a success …

is not pure …

is pure …

does not win over conceit …

wins over conceit …

does not grow in wisdom …

grows in wisdom …

makes much bad karma …

makes much merit.

What ten?

Right view, right thought, right speech, right action, right livelihood, right effort, right mindfulness, right immersion, right knowledge, and right freedom.

A person who has these ten qualities makes much merit."